CHEAP ADVICE

Cheap Advice

CALVERT DEFOREST

WITH

DOUG MCINTYRE
PHILIPPE RUSKIN
AND
BRIAN CURY

WARNER BOOKS

A Time Warner Company

WARNER BOOKS
A Time Warner Company

Warner Books, Inc., 1271 Avenue of the Americas, New York, NY 10020

A Time Warner Company

Printed in the United States of America

First Printing: December 1994

10 9 8 7 6 5 4 3 2 1

Library of Congress Cataloging-in-Publication Data

DeForest, Calvert
Cheap advice : a guide to low-cost luxery / Calvert DeForest with Doug McIntyre, Philippe Ruskin, and Brian Cury.
p. cm.
ISBN 0-446-67082-0
1. Success--Humor. 2. Self-help techniques--Humor. I. Title.
PN6231.S83D44 1994
818'.5402--dc20 94-26522
CIP

Cover design by Julia Kushnirsky

Cover photograph by Michael Grecco

Book design by H. Roberts Design

Illustrations by Peter M. Morlock except for . . .
Howard Roberts's illustrations and special computer effects appearing on pages vii, 2, 4, 9, 11, 12, 17, 20, 23, 24, 26, 39, 42, 46, 47, 58, 62, 66, 70, 77, 88 and 95.

Photos by James Daley except for . . .
Photos provided by UPI/BETTMAN and THE BETTMANN ARCHIVE on pages 7, 8, 12, 28, 59, 60, 67, 68 and 69
Photos by Andrew Levin on pages 17 and 46
Photo courtesy of U.S. concepts Inc./Aspen Comedy Festival on page 54

Contents

Acknowledgments

aniele Diane Christine Judy Jennifer Michael Guy Beverly Lauren Dawn Shelley Lillian Melissa Brian Howar
elen Graham Mauro Kally Kinsey Diana Mel Karen Susan Donato Gelsomina Vinko Adriana Marina Jonatha
hn Donna Christine Greg Diana Joy Maria Joe Dana Greggie Flora Lew Manlio Laurie Nicholas Angelo Pete
ack Alina Scarlett Jasmine Ian Barbara William Ray Elsa Danny Richie Peter Irene Paul Carla Petey Beba
my Frank Chuck Robin Ari Lauren Charles Claire Tom Bruce Chris Benjamin Alexander Steve Maxine Rob
ren Shirley Lenny Sharon Norma Julie Milton Philly Daniele Diane Christine Judy Jennifer Michael Guy Be
Lauren Dawn Shelley Lillian Melissa Brian Howard Helen Ian Barbara William Graham Mauro Kally Kins
ana Mel Karen Susan Donato Gelsomina Vinko Adriana Marina Jonathan John Donna Christine Greg Diana J
aria Joe Dana Greggie Flora Lew Manlio Laurie Nicholas Angelo Peter Jack Alina Scarlett Jasmine Ray El
Danny Richie Peter Irene Paul Carla Petey Beba Jimmy Frank Chuck Robin Ari Lauren Charles Claire Tom
ruce Chris Benjamin Alexander Steve Maxine Robin Lauren Lenny Sharon Norma Julie Milton Philly Daniele
Diane Christine Judy Jennifer Michael Guy Beverly Lauren Dawn Shelley Lillian Ian Barbara William Melissa
Brian Howard Helen Graham Mauro Kally Kinsey Diana Mel Karen Susan Donato Gelsomina Vinko Adriana
Marina Jonathan John Donna Christine Greg Diana Joy Maria Joe Dana Greggie Flora Lew Manlio Laurie
holas Angelo Peter Jack Alina Scarlett Jasmine Ray Elsa Ian Barbara William Danny Richie Peter Irene P
rla Petey Beba Jimmy Frank Chuck Robin Ari Lauren Ian Barbara William Charles Claire Tom Bruce Chr
jamin Alexander Steve Maxine Robin Lauren Lenny Sharon Norma Julie Milton Philly Daniele Diane Christi
udy Jennifer Michael Guy Beverly Lauren Dawn Shelley Lillian Melissa Brian Howard Helen Graham Mauro
ally Kinsey Diana Mel Karen Susan Donato Gelsomina Vinko Adriana Marina Jonathan John Donna Christine
Diana Joy Maria Joe Dana Greggie Flora Lew Manlio Laurie Nicholas Angelo Peter Jack Alina Scarlett J
mine Ray Elsa Danny Richie Peter Irene Paul Carla Petey Beba Ian Barbara William Jimmy Frank Chuck
Robin Ari Lauren Charles Claire Tom Bruce Chris Benjamin Alexander Steve Maxine Robin Lauren Lenny
ron Norma Julie Milton Philly Daniele Diane Christine Judy Jennifer Michael Guy Beverly Lauren Dawn Sh

MEMORANDUM

TO: The ignorant, uninformed, unhappy, dazed, confused, gullible. In other words, my fans everywhere.

FROM: Calvert DeForest, Esq.
Chairman of the Board & CEO
Cal-Co® Industries, Incorporated

Dear Reader,[1]

Congratulations! You are now the proud owner of what may be the finest self-help book ever written in the English language. CALVERT DeFOREST'S BOOK OF CHEAP ADVICE is not one of those hastily thrown together rip-offs that gravitate to the frat-house crapper. This is a painstakingly crafted rip-off that will be an honored addition to any home or office library.

Most books nowadays are printed on acid-free paper. Not my book. With my book you not only get all the acid of regular paper, but as an added bonus, I've thrown in 25 percent more acid than paper should even have![2] Any butthead can see that's a bargain.

CALVERT DeFOREST'S BOOK OF CHEAP ADVICE is made by Americans, for Americans. Each of you should consider it your patriotic duty to keep it that way. Once my book has swept the nation, America will be healthier, smarter, richer, even prettier! Don't let this book fall into the hands of foreign nationals or paid lobbyists for foreign powers. Why should Canada, for instance, get the benefits of my lifetime of work? It's bad enough they've been cowering behind our nuclear umbrella all these years. Now they come crying to me to help them fix their personal, financial, and romantic problems? HA! The bacon-munching, hockey-fetished,

tiny-armied hosers with a couple of good brands of beer and no stereo and hi-fi industry . . . I think I've made my point.

A healthy and happy country is a powerful country. If you want to keep America the unstoppable military juggernaut that she is, then read this book, memorize it, burn it; buy another one and burn that too. The information contained within these pages is classified TOP SECRET. Don't you become the weak link in America's nation security chain.

God bless you all, and God bless the United States of America.

Calvert DeForest, Esq.
Chairman of the Board & CEO

Cal-Co® Industries, Incorporated

1. Applies only to paying readers. You book-voyeurs who read in the store and then put the book back on the shelf—who needs you!
2. Cal-Co® is the world's leading manufacturer of poisonous acids.

Introduction

When I decided to write an advice book, cynics—damn them all!—questioned my qualifications. While it's true I'm not a doctor or a lawyer, or allowed to live in Oklahoma City without notifying the police department, I have lived the lives of ten men. I have been in the arena, bloodying my hands with the ugly work that must be done so that you people can sleep soundly in your beds at night.

I am Everyman. I am your friend, your neighbor. I'm the doctor who told you to turn your head and cough. I am a symbol of your highest hopes; I'm your worst nightmare if you cross me or fail to pay gambling debts.

While it's true that compared to my life (a whirlwind of excitement that's seen me go through money and other men's wives like so many cans of Beef-A-Roni) your life will seem like a criminal waste of DNA—take heart! I'm giving you the chance to live vicariously through me, reaping the rewards of all my wisdom. Not bad for $8.99.

Read on! Read on! Seek the light of truth, for it shall set you free.

CALVERT DeFOREST

84 KENNEDY STREET
HACKENSACK, NEW JERSEY 07601
1-900-SUCKERS

Current Position
Chairman of the Board and CEO,
Cal-Co® Industries, Incorporated

Career Goals
256*
*Ranks 14th in NHL History

Previous Experience

1941-1945	War Protester
1946	Went "All the Way" for First Time
1950	Invented Slam Dunk
1951-1966	Corrupt Mayor of Erie, Pennsylvania
1960	Tossed out of Rat Pack by Pissed-off Peter Lawford
1963	Security Director, Texas School Book Depository
1968-1969	Backup Drummer for Cream
1972-1979	Assistant Director of CIA
1974	Found Birth Parents
1975	Cleared of War Crimes
1979	Partner, Rose Law Firm—Little Rock, Arkansas
1985	Project Director, NASA—*Challenger* Mission
1986-1988	Steve of Steve and Eydie
1993	Creative Consultant, *The Chevy Chase Show*
1994	Midseason Coach Replacement, New York Knicks

Education
1933-1946 James K. Polk High School, Brooklyn, New York

Personal Information
A bachelor, gourmand, notary public, Elk, and last known member of the Whig party, Calvert lives a nomadic life with his twin Siberian tigers, Sigfried and Ebbert.

Getting Rich

Cheap Ways to Get Rich Quick

I believe it was Ben Franklin who said "There's a sucker born every minute." In today's information superhighway age, that means ten thousand born every minute, and today's suckers have telephones: car phones, cellular phones, cordless phones. The boobs not only have phones, they've also got credit cards. Think about that for a minute. Millions of saps are out there right now living their dreary lives in abject despair. Perhaps the only thing standing between them and a .38 to the temple is a two-dollar-a-minute call to one of Cal-Co's® many 900 chat lines.

I don't like to brag, but my Chat Line division has raked in profits that would make Oprah blush. Here are some really cheap suggestions for those of you who want to break into this lucrative industry and make some real money right away:

1-900-HOOKERS®
Daily updates for anglers. For two dollars a minute, fishermen get up-to-the-second information on the hottest fishing spots in their area. Boring, you say? Of course it is! But here's the catch: Thousands of out-of-state horny businessmen with per diems will call thinking they can get a twenty-two-year-old tramp in a fishnet dress sent to their hotel. What are they gonna do, complain? HA! HA! HA! Suckers!

1-900-PET TALK®
Do you like to tell endless stories about the cute thing your cat did last week? Of course not; you've got a life! But think of the millions out there who babble on endlessly about Fifi or Fluffy and what they did with a piece of yarn. 1-900-PET TALK is a nationwide party line for dog and cat owners. Don't underestimate the gullibility of the pet-owning public. You can sell these suckers anything.

1-900-HOLD PLZ®
This one's a beauty. For two dollars a minute callers hear "Hold please." That's it. There's nothing more to it. We don't even play a crappy version of "You Are the Sunshine of My Life" while they wait. They just call up and you stick 'em on hold. There's no hassle of updating daily messages—or even having a message! 1-900-HOLD PLZ will make you rich quick.

1-900-NIRVANA®
Old hippies and young New Age Zen-heads will fill up your cash drawer calling in hoping for the keys to a happier life. What they'll hear instead is an endless loop of Kurt Cobain's song lyrics read by Ed Asner.

1-900-IDIOTS®
This number automatically transfers the caller to 1-900-HOLD PLZ. The beauty part is, you can double bill them. Again, in three years, not one complaint.

1-900-PIZZAS®
A restaurant? Nope. A delivery service? Nope. 1-900-PIZZAS is the nation's first pizza-lovers' chat line. Fat pigs from coast to coast call in to tell each other how much they like pizza, which topping is their favorite, and how many slices they can eat without blowing a hole in their aorta.

1-900-ARSENIO®
Fans of the canceled late-night gab show host don't have to go without their daily fix of Arsenio's wit and wisdom. Each day they'll hear a different hilarious Arsenio Hall monologue, including plenty of fist-waving political commentary like "Dan Quayle is a jerk." Weekly surprise guests include Sinbad, Malcolm Jamal-Warner, Whoopi, and Louis Farrakhan.

Really Cheap Ways to Get Rid of Your Boss

- Send him memos printed on asbestos stationery.
- Do something really stupid that ruins the company. Sure, you'll lose your job, but so will he!
- Car bomb.
- Send a bimbo to his hotel room in Little Rock. Call a press conference to announce a lawsuit.
- Call the *Times* and leak his name as the key witness to a gangland slaying.
- Show up early for work; move all your stuff into his office. When he shows up, fire him!
- Send him a phony telegram from Ed McMahon telling him he's won a million dollars. Wait for him to tell off his boss and quit.
- Convince your boss that the public will go crazy for a book of cheap advice.
- Quit.

Calvert DeForest's Three Golden Rules of Business

Money. God, I love the stuff!

Unless you've got something wrong with your brain, you love money too. And that's a good thing, because this world is a cruel and ugly place when you don't have piles of cash hanging around the house. I'm not talking about a couple of grand, I'm talking about stacks and stacks of loot. Millions. Are you getting the picture?

Okay, I can hear you out there whining, "That's easy for you to say, Cal . . . You're a handsome and fabulously successful tycoon who's also cheap and still has the first dime he ever swindled." All that's true. But you caught me on a good day, so I'm going to share some of my secrets to amassing a great big fat fortune.

Cal's Three Golden Rules of Business

RULE 1: THINK OF SOMETHING PEOPLE WANT.

RULE 2: MAKE IT CHEAP.

RULE 3: SELL IT FOR A LOT.

Will everybody buy it? Not necessarily, but if you charge enough you won't have to sell it to everybody. When it comes to pricing, go for it! The "meek might inherit the earth," but if you follow "Cal's Three Golden Rules of Business," they'll have to inherit it from you!

Dear Cal,

Recently I took over a successful business. For thirty years it ran like a well-oiled machine. At first, everything seemed okay. Then this new guy opened up a similar business right next door. Now, sales are terrible. I don't know what I should do. Any suggestions?

J. Leno
Burbank, CA

From the desk of Calvert DeForest

Dear Mr. Leno,

Having never failed at anything, I don't think I'm really qualified to answer your question. However, I do know of an excellent organization that may be able to help. Talk Show Hosts Anonymous is a twelve-step program for unwatchable talk show hosts. Meetings are held on a regular basis at 11:30 P.M.* If you're interested, there's one tonight at Chevy's house.

Good luck,

* Reservations suggested due to recent overbooking.

Office Party Etiquette

There's nothing like waking up the day after an office party with that sinking, nervous, nauseous feeling that perhaps you might have made one trip too many to the punch bowl and said a few things that would have been better off left unsaid.

Here are some invaluable tips to remember next time the boss breaks out the cheap champagne:

- It's okay to tell the boss what a great time you're having at this "lovely get-together." It's not okay to tell the boss, "The beer's warm and you're a pig-faced prick who wouldn't know a good employee from a hole in the ground!"
- Don't brag about how many days you've left before five.
- If there is an attractive employee you really like, this may be the time to ask him/her out. However, if turned down, never shout "Screw you; you're fired!"
- Don't Xerox your butt until after the boss leaves the party.
- Never puke into the file cabinet.
- If you mean to tell your boss of twenty years to please pass the dip, be careful not to make this classic Freudian slip: "You rat bastard, you ruined my life!"
- Don't approach the boss's wife and ask her to "pull my finger."
- If you missed fifteen weeks of work because of a job-related back injury, remember to stay off the dance floor when they play "Shout!"
- Tonight's not the night for that see-through blouse.

Calvert's Guide to Making Money

I'm a very rich man. You're not. Study my guide to money and maybe, someday, you too will be a robber baron like me.

Cal's Quick Tip

Want to make a quick million? Clip out these bills, pick up some green paper, and have yourself a blast on the office Xerox machine!

The $100,000.00 Bill

She's a beauty, all right. Pretty to look at and soft to the touch, but forget about getting change at the 7-11! Back in the go-go eighties, when America still had balls, 100G notes were tossed around like frisbees. Today, in the "less is more" nineties, the $100,000 bill is considered déclassé. Don't despair, though, what goes around comes around. I'm keeping my Woody Wilsons and my fur coats.

The $10,000.00 Bill

Now we're talking cash. The 10G note is perfect for fleeing the country. A one-way ticket to the Cayman Islands.

The $5,000.00 Bill

The perfect denomination for Vegas. A fistful of these and you're *getting* that front row seat at Siegfried and Roy's dinner show. Think your housekeeper might be ripping you off? Drop a couple of Jimmy Madisons around the house and see if they disappear. . . . Then fire her ass!

The $1,000.00 Bill

You can have a lot of fun with the G note. The other day I'm walking down Broadway, the street of dreams, when this bum stumbles up and asks for a handout. I pull out a thousand, give it to him, and watch his face light up. Then I yank it back out of his filthy paw and toss him a dime. HA! HA! HA!

The $100.00 Bill

These are really more trouble than they're worth. So, as a service to my faithful readers, I'm willing to take them off your hands. Mail your hundred-dollar bills to: Calvert DeForest c/o Cal-Co® Industries. I will personally dispose of every C note that comes through the door.

The $50.00 Bill

You may have seen this one. The fifty is pretty common among "thousandairs." Personally, I haven't used it in years. Still, I'm told the fifty is accepted at grocery stores, gas stations, prizefights, and traffic court. So, if you have a fifty, by all means spend it.

The $20.00 Bill

Lord, Andrew Jackson has a long face! And look at that hair, will you? Who does he think he is, the Beast from *Beauty and the Beast*? The twenty is a tight little package that looks good when you drop it in the collection plate at church on Sunday, and it's perfect for the neighborhood punk who shovels your driveway when it snows. By all means, keep a pile of twenties around the house at all times.

The $10.00 Bill

It's just not as good as the twenty. In fact, you'd have to give me *two* tens for a twenty. That's just how I feel about it. Now, Alexander Hamilton I like. He practically invented money. If only that rat bastard John Wilkes Booth hadn't shot him.

The $5.00 Bill

Lincoln Schminkin! The five is a waste of paper. Just throw them out.

The $1.00 Bill

It's like a paper penny. Would you bend down to pick one off the street? Not me, pal. The dollar, when stacked into bundles, is perfect for jamming under a wobbly sofa. I use them to light kindling up at my ski chalet. The greenback is also a good teaching aide to use when you're explaining poverty to youngsters. Ben Franklin said it best: "A dollar saved is a dollar earned."

Cheap Tips for Saving Money

- Steal everything.
- Mooch off friends.
- Move back home with Mom and Dad.
- Clip those coupons!
- Metal detectors aren't just for the beach anymore.
- Panhandle between classes.
- Did I mention stealing?

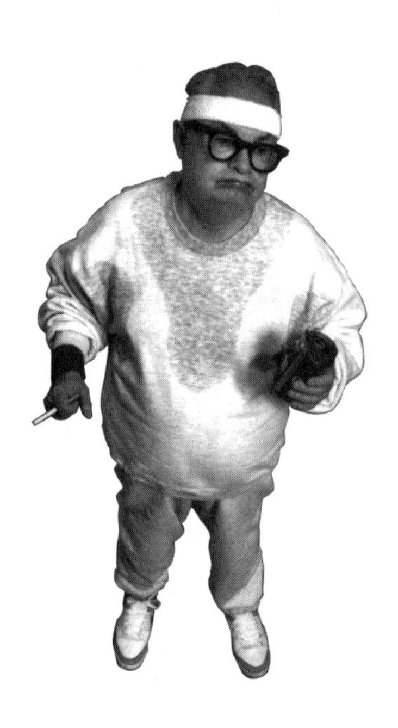

Health & Fitness

Old
Butts

Health and Fitness

I think it was four-time Indy champ A. J. Foyt who said, "The human body is the temple of the soul."

Finding the perfect balance between the proper diet and an effective exercise regime has become a national obsession. Jane Fonda went from communist sympathizer to iron-buttocked fitness guru, all because you couldn't lay off the Dove bars or get up from the sofa to switch from *Regis and Kathy Lee* to *Beavis and Butthead*. I hope you're proud of your flabby selves.

Unlike most health and fitness guides, mine comes with no disclaimers. I guarantee that if you follow my recommendations in the areas of diet and exercise, your body will end up looking EXACTLY like mine!

Eat Right the DeForest Way!

For most of us, breakfast is the first meal of the day. And like your first at-bat in the majors or your first sexual encounter, it's important that it be an enjoyable experience and not involve your uncle.

So, start the day off right with a healthy breakfast. Pancakes, waffles, chicken-fried steak with white gravy and biscuits, maybe a side of Canadian bacon with cheese grits . . . Knock yourself out! Go for it! The world is an ugly place. You could get slaughtered by a gang of punks on your way to work. So, do what I do. Eat every meal as if it were your last. One of these days, it's gonna be. HA! HA! HA!

Breakfast Recipe

Cal's Puffy Omelet

6 eggs, separated
6 tablespoons water
1 teaspoon salt
1/8 teaspoon pepper
2 tablespoons butter
14 oz. bourbon

Preheat oven to 350°. Take a small mixing bowl and beat egg whites with water and salt until stiff peaks form when beaters are lifted. Crank up the gas and stick it on the stove. Run to the liquor cabinet and get a bottle of good domestic bourbon. Pour three healthy glugs of bourbon into a tumbler. Toss back the bourbon and return the frying pan to the flame for five minutes. Use a spatula to remove the omelet from the pan. Pour two more glugs of bourbon into a fresh tumbler and toss that back. The effects of two big belts of booze at eight in the morning will more than offset any errors you may have made in the kitchen with a couple of crappy eggs.

This is an old-time family favorite around the DeForest household. Enjoy!

Lunch

Lunch is a misunderstood meal. It's not just the midday repast; it's an opportunity to hit on the boss's secretary, to drink on the company's dime, and it's a forum for you to grouse about working conditions with coworkers who then return to the office with lowered morale. In other words, lunch is the subversive meal. For this reason, Cal-Co® Industries has led the charge in eliminating the lunch hour completely. By preventing our employees from eating during the day, we have made Cal-Co®'s staff leaner and meaner. Exactly the kind of workforce America's gonna need if we expect to kick ass in the new Global Village economy. So, if you own a company yourself, or are responsible for a workforce of any size, take a page from Cal-Co®'s book and send out your own "Screw Lunch" memo today.

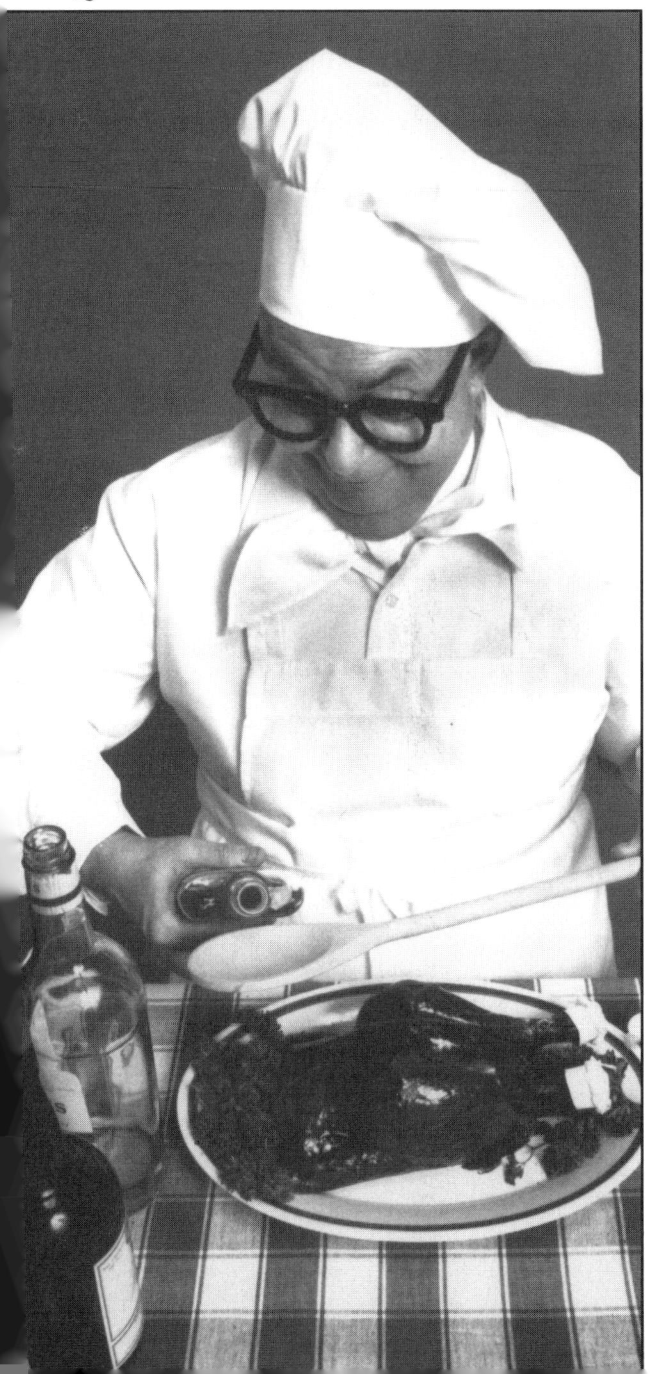

Lunch Recipe

Cal's Famous Baked Clubhouse Sandwiches

4 slices bread, toasted
1 quart single malt scotch whiskey
4 large slices chicken
4 large slices ham
1 bowl beer nuts
1 can condensed cream of mushroom soup
1/4 cup dry sherry
paprika

Preheat oven to 375°. In baking pan, arrange toast in a single layer. Top with slices of chicken and ham. Mix cream of mushroom soup with dry sherry. Pour over top of chicken/ham/toast. Sprinkle with paprika, then bake for twenty minutes. This serves four.

If you really want to please the kids, instead of sherry, empty a full bottle of imported single malt scotch into soup. It kills the flavor completely, but it also takes the edge off your post-breakfast hangover and quiets teething children.

Dear Mr. DeForest,
I'm a young mother who wants to feed her family only natural foods that are both healthy and delicious.

As an environmentalist I'm opposed to chemical additives. Can you suggest something that will please both my kids and the earth?

Ms. Lizbeth Brinkley
Mendecino, CA

From the desk of Calvert DeForest

Dear Ms. Brinkley,

Let me start by assuring you that Cal-Co® shares your love of the environment. After all, some of our best-selling products are made from nature. This includes, of course, Cal-Co®'s OWLS ON A STICK. OWLS ON A STICK® are made from 100 percent pure Northern Spotted Owl. Each owl is low in fat, high in vitamins, and easy to eat thanks to the patented tropical rain forest stick jabbed into each bird. And let me remind you, Ms. Brinkley, Cal-Co® uses only USDA-approved *American* owls, not cheap foreign imports mixed with artificial fillers and additives. You can rest assured that only the best-tasting, lip-smacking, tummy-pleasing owl meat will reach your dinner plate.

Sincerely,

CAL

Calvert DeForest
CEO, Cal-Co® Industries

Dinner

Dinner is family time. Time for the whole clan to gather together at the table, break bread, and share their day's adventures. It's the time of day when tiny little scabs get picked at until they open up into gushing, hemorrhaging rivers of pent-up resentment and hurt.

Dinner is a hastily thrown together mishmash of prepackaged microwaveable oriental-style vegetables and flash-frozen cod squares.

Dinner is the time of day your son chooses to come out of the closet. It's when your daughter announces she's having your brother-in-law's child. It's the meal Dad's never sober for; the meal Mom quietly sobs through.

Obviously, a meal with this much bad karma attached could be a dieter's nightmare. So it's important to keep your eye on the prize. This starts with the choice of the dinner table itself. I've found an all-glass table is an excellent aide to reducing your caloric intake. Try putting on a pair of shorty-shorts and pulling your chair real close to the table's edge. The sight of your pasty thighs staring back in your face from just below your plate should be enough to make anyone pass on a second helping of macaroni and cheese.

If you've got the stomach for it, try eating completely naked. I did this once and it put me off my feed for weeks. A great way to drop some extra pounds in a hurry.

Dinner Recipe

Cal's Basic Pot Roast

meat
vermouth
gin
cocktail onions

In a flarge pry fan, brown meat on both sides in hot oil for about fifteen minutes which is enough time to stir up more of those dilicious martini's I like so very mush. . . . Add water (ugh!) pepper; hell, put in some Drano and bacon grease if you want. God love ya! You're a hell of a great guy and I love ya. Love ya like a brothers. . . . Throw in some more ingredamints. Did I tell you to turn on the stove? Well, you have to turn on the stove. That should be prddy obvious to anybdy. Where'd I put that dnk? dammit! Who swipped my drink?! Screw you! Screw the f$#king pot f$#king roast! Geez, I hate ta cook; letsh order a pizzha!

HA!
HA!
HA!

Staying Fit

Everybody knows that if you want to get in shape in the nineties you have to drop a couple of grand a year in some La-De-Da fancy health club. Before you humiliate yourself in public by squeezing into a pair of spandex bicycle pants that make you look like a Denny's Grand Slam breakfast link sausage, I suggest you study my handy Guide to Health Club Dos and Don'ts.

DO use the StairMaster if your butt sags below your knees.
DON'T use the StairMaster if you lost a leg in a hunting accident.

DO warm up before working out. The sound of snapping tendons is distracting to other health club members.
DON'T warm up by eating a bowl of three-alarm chili.

DO wipe perspiration off the exercise equipment after each use.
DON'T bottle the perspiration and sell it as Roseanne's new scent for women.

DO flirt with the cute guy on the treadmill next to you.
DON'T flirt if his tattoo reads "666."

DO drink plenty of liquids.
DON'T eat tuna fish in the sauna.

DO take off your beeper before showering.
DON'T wear a Speedo bathing suit in public if you've ever said, "Jumbo pizza with everything on it."

DO remember to smile if you make eye contact with someone attractive.
DON'T shout, "Hey, Grizzly Adams!" at the Turkish girl doing leg lifts.

MINNOW

Travel

Really Cheap Travel Tips

Call it wanderlust, the lure of the open road, the call of the sea, the erotic possibilities of a first-class upgrade. There's a lot more to travel, however, than just trying to score with a stewardess. If you don't know what to expect, some countries can be a real drag to visit. For instance, Italy. Forget about trying to make heads or tails out of that money they use over there. And what's the story with that gibberish they speak in France? Haven't those clowns ever heard of English?

To help you chart a safe course through this big wonderful round ball of a planet called earth, I've committed to paper a few helpful hints for travelers, both foreign and domestic. Don't leave home without it!

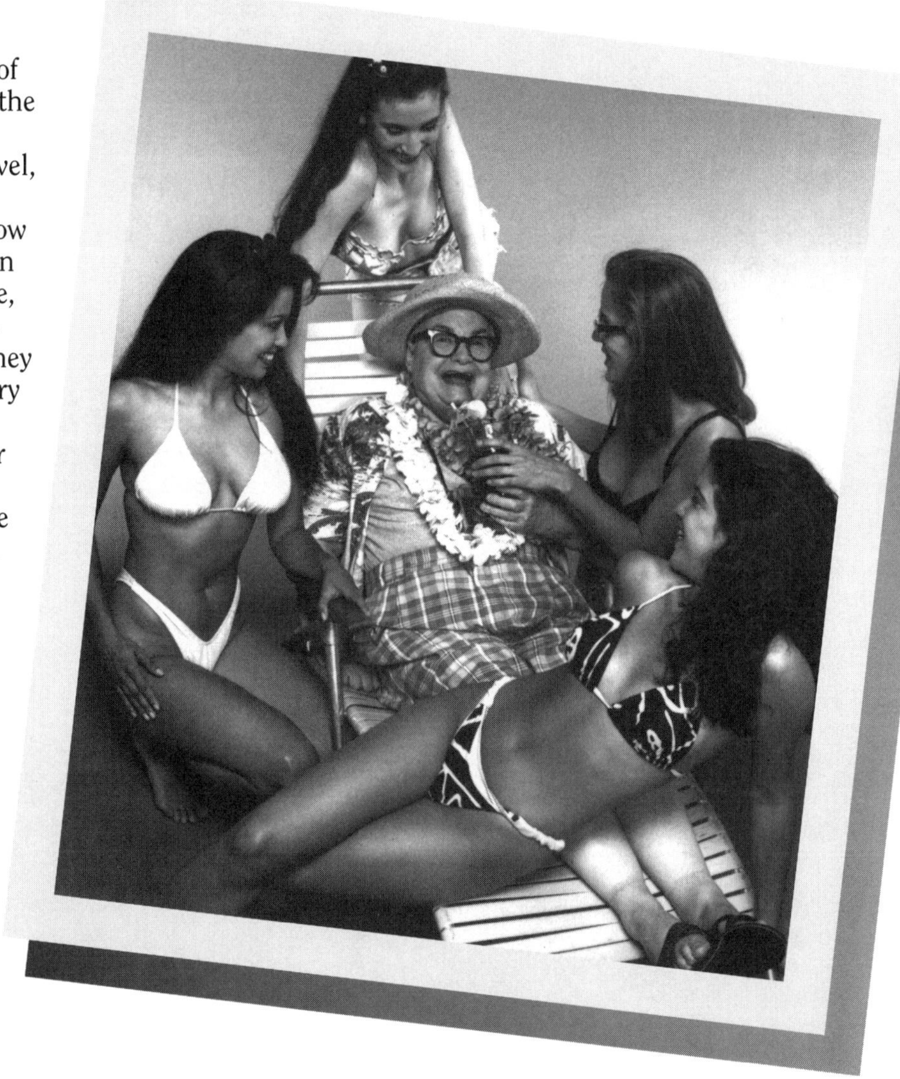

FOREIGN TRAVEL

- Hookers are cheaper in Vietnam, but cleaner in Holland.
- When in Germany, try not to mention Hitler.
- When in France, feel free to skip out on your hotel bill. If they whine about it tell them to take it off their war debt.
- When in Japan, try to remind them that our cars might suck but our bombs are fantastic!
- If you get arrested while visiting in Mexico, don't offer the guard Arizona and California if he'll let you go. Apparently, they're on to this one.
- Under no circumstances should you spray-paint parked cars in Singapore.
- Remember, opening an IRA account doesn't mean the same thing in Belfast as it does here in the States.
- Want to visit Poland? Save yourself a lot of bread and a long plane ride. Drive to West Virginia and I'll bet you ten grand you'll never know the difference.
- Sarajevo is cheaper during sniper season, but more colorful during the mortar festival.

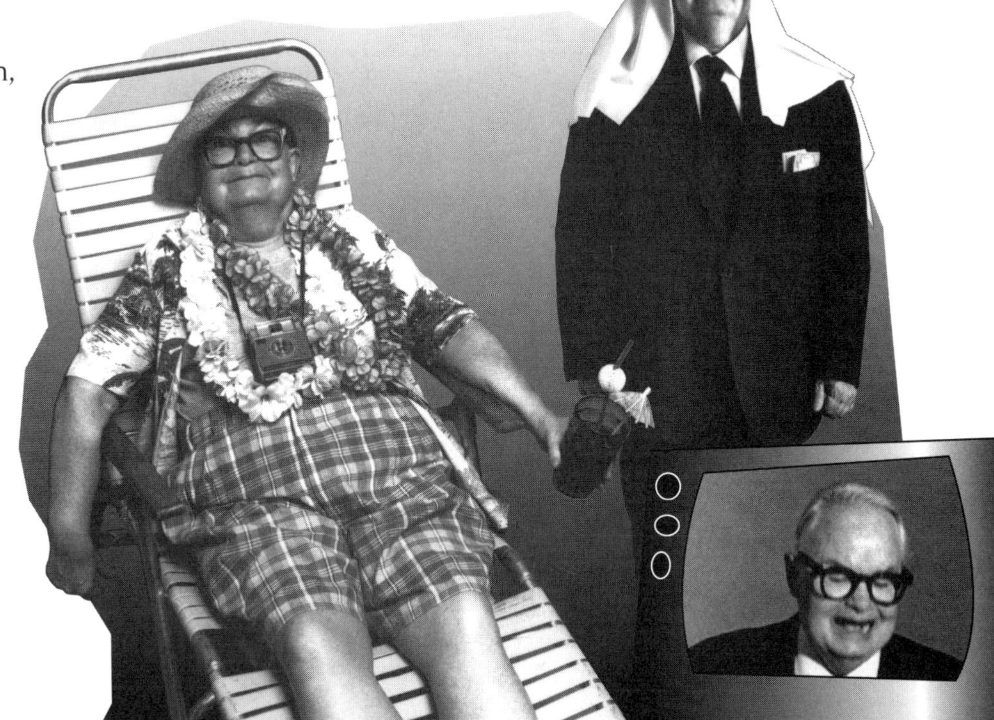

DOMESTIC TRAVEL

- When in Atlanta, don't say anything like "For my money Sherman didn't go far enough!
- In Florida, doughnuts are nouvelle cuisine.
- When visiting New Hampshire, make sure you see the Negro.
- In Boston, it's okay to slander America, insult God, but always genuflect when talking about the Celtics.
- The four food groups in Alabama are: grease, sugar, booze, and tobacco.
- In Los Angeles the air comes in two popular flavors: Regular and Extra Chunky.
- If you want to stretch the food budget when traveling in Oklahoma, remember: Road kill is always better the second day.

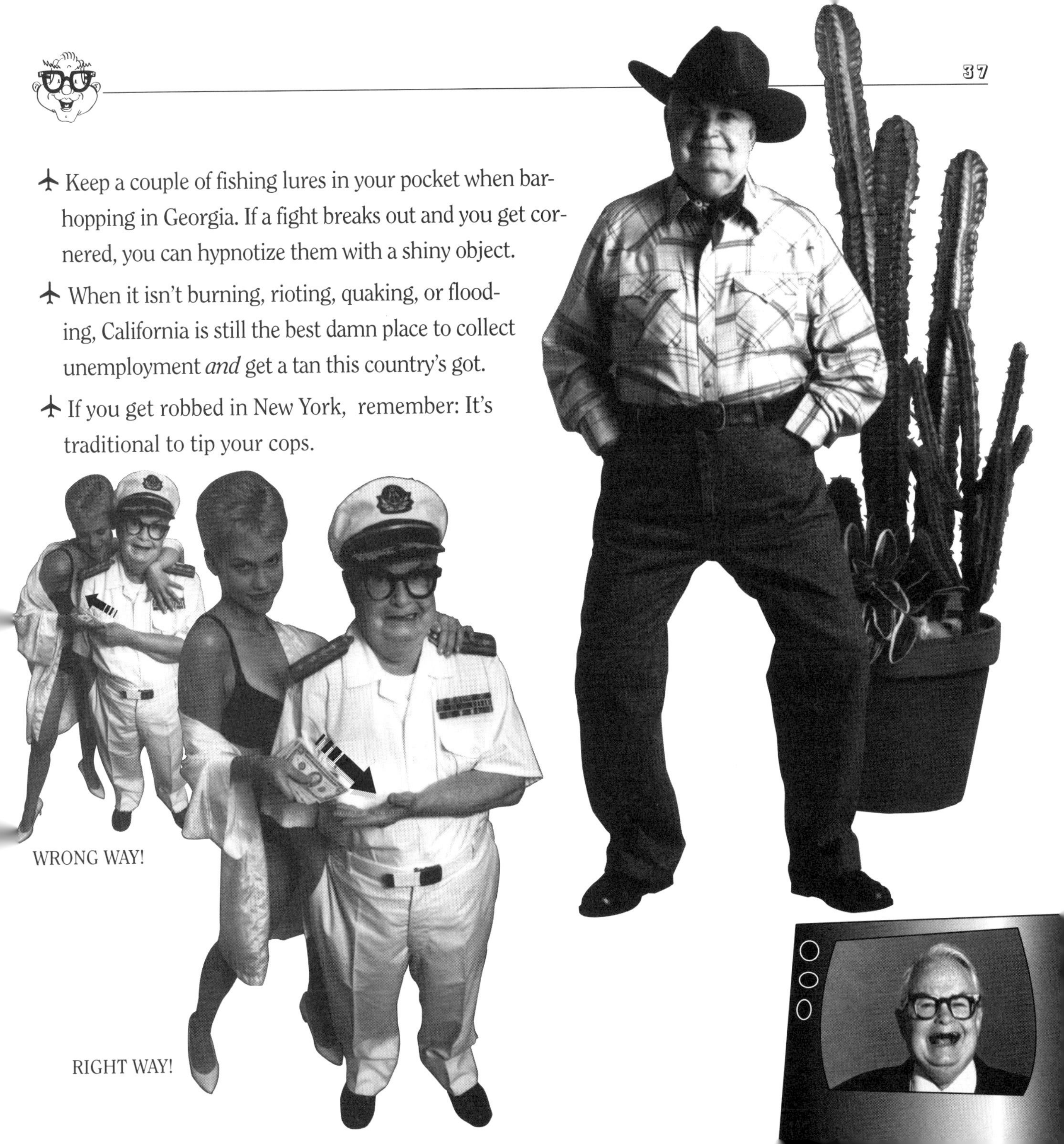

- Keep a couple of fishing lures in your pocket when bar-hopping in Georgia. If a fight breaks out and you get cornered, you can hypnotize them with a shiny object.
- When it isn't burning, rioting, quaking, or flooding, California is still the best damn place to collect unemployment *and* get a tan this country's got.
- If you get robbed in New York, remember: It's traditional to tip your cops.

TO BE, OR NOT TO BE...

VERY IMPRESSIVE, MISTER DEFOREST!! YOU'VE GOT THE JOB!!!

Show Biz

How to Get That Hollywood Look (cheap)

HAIR TREATMENT: Formerly known as a haircut.

SHADES: (Sunglasses, to you civilians) Wear them morning, noon and night, rain or shine. If you bump into people, tell them to get out of the way!

GOLD CHAIN: I use the word "gold" loosely here. Make sure it looks real, doesn't turn black in the rain or melt in sunlight.

RED RIBBON: Any card store carries ribbon. Just bring along some handy scissors and discreetly clip what you need. Hey, you're doing it for a good cause!

CIGAR: The bigger the better.

SCREENPLAY: Been carrying it around since your sophomore year of college? With a brand new binder, no one will tell the difference.

PINKY RING: Kids shouldn't be wearing jewelry. A child's ring should fit your pinky. (You do the math.)

SPORTS JACKET: Go to an Armani boutique. Rip out the brand name tag from one of those fancy suits. Sew it into your Wal-Mart special.

JEANS: You don't need to tear any gashes. All the groveling and kneeling will wear these out quickly enough.

. . . Or simply emulate your favorite star!

How to Make It Big in Show Business

Being a highly paid star isn't always the stroll in the sun it appears to be. There's an ugly side that comes with all the fame and glitter. You've got agents and managers and PR hacks. . . . There's that cesspool of loose women and gay pool boys known as Hollywood. . . . And let's not forget *you* people, the fickle public. You love me one minute, then forget about me like last week's lunch. Screw you! I saved my money; I don't need anybody!

Sorry.

If you have delusions of fame in this business called show, study these next few pages carefully. My guide to success in the entertainment industry will keep you on the path to success and off a badly stained casting couch in Van Nuys.

How to Handle Critics

Dear Calvert,

Recently I appeared as Willy Loman in my high school production of Death of a Salesman. I was stung by the bitter and brutal review I received at the hands of the school paper's theater critic. Mr. Ortega is well known for his poison pen and open hostility to American playwrights. Still, I think he was way out of line when he wrote, "Alan Mruvka really bit the big one as Willy Loman."

Frankly, Mr. DeForest, I can barely walk the halls at school without being taunted by these ugly words. Tell me how you deal with the pain caused by hateful critics.

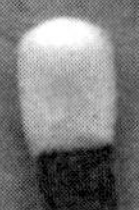

Alan Mruvka
Los Angeles, California

From the desk of Calvert DeForest

Dear Alan,

I believe it was me who said, "Critics suck!" I was, as usual, correct. Those who can, do. Those who can't, write for the ***Times***. Unlike many public figures (Clinton), I don't let the naysayers get me down. If I had a dime for every time someone told me I was terrible, awful, lousy, rotten, stupid, ugly, dumb, goofy, a jerk. . . . Well, I think you get the point.

The world has always had critics, and I suppose it always will. (Unless, of course, I get my hands on real power, in which case—labor camps!) But I digress. It's important to remember that there is almost nothing they can say about you that can't be spun to your advantage. For example, some of the early reviews of this book were a little less than flattering. However, with a nip here and a tuck there, angry words became dust jacket blurbs . . .

***The Los Angeles Times* said:**

"CHEAP ADVICE is a crime against nature. To think that Warner Books would publish this waste of paper is simply astonishing!"

Now, I take my magic pencil, and presto!

CHEAP ADVICE is . . . simply astonishing!

***The Christian Science Monitor* said:**

"Calvert DeForest's CHEAP ADVICE is a full-frontal assault on the English language. DeForest an author? Don't make me laugh! Not only would I be willing to bet a year's salary he didn't write this book; I'd bet two more years' salary he's never even read a book!"

Obviously, a review like that is going to kill sales if anyone gets wind of it. So, by scratching out an unnecessary word here and there, the Christian Science Monitor *becomes my best friend. . . .*

Calvert DeForest . . . make(s) me laugh!

The New York Times, those liberal bastards, have always been jealous of my success. Look what they tried to say about me:

"The Hindenberg, the space shuttle ***Challenger,*** the Bush/Quayle campaign; move over and make room for the grandest, greatest, most spectacular tragedy of them all! Calvert DeForest's CHEAP ADVICE will set back the cause of literacy and culture a thousand years. It's crammed with errors, and there isn't an original idea to be found within its flimsy one-hundred-and-four pages. Those who are foolish enough to buy this 'book' will feel cheated, ripped off, insulted, demeaned, and so many other negative emotions, the suicide hotline will have to add a second switchboard."

Here's what The New York Times *is going to say:*

"... the grandest, greatest, most spectacular ... (book). Will ... cause literacy and culture. It's crammed with ... original idea(s). Those who ... buy this book will feel ... emotions. ..."

So, if you get two thumbs down from the critics, give them a couple of fingers right back. I'll be tap dancing all the way to the bank, all thanks to their unqualified raves. Suckers! HA! HA! HA!

CAL

Cal Before Makeup

Cal After Makeup

Good TV Movie Ideas

Country western singer's abusive marriage ends in murder/suicide.

Hideously painful incurable epidemic sweeps through big city housing project. Bush administration conspiracy blamed.

Two young boys from broken homes change the world for the better, while learning to stand on their own.

High-priced call girls turn the tables on international drug cartel.

Obsessed fan stalks and slays popular soap opera star, then lands a role on the same soap opera.

Cindy Crawford's sex diary.

Bad TV Movie Ideas

Richard Pryor's barbecue secrets.

The county sewer commission approves a nine-million-dollar rural development project.

A cute little duck swims around in a pond for two hours.

Asian family arrives in America, works very hard in small neighborhood shop. They save their money and move from a crime-infested city to a safe suburb. Kids do well in school.

Guy wins lottery and handles newfound riches with dignity and intelligence.

Bea Arthur's sex diary.

Take the following multiple choice show biz quiz to see if you have what it takes to make it on the A list in Hollywood:

1. You're up for a tiny role in a low-budget slasher flick. The director asks you to meet him in a cheap motel room to discuss the part. You . . .

A) Go alone.
B) Go with a friend.
C) Go with a friend, a video camera, and a bottle of baby oil.
D) Go with your lawyer.

ANSWER: C—A tiny role is better than no role.

2. You've been with your agent for five years. During that time, you've never netted less than 300K a year. The new TV season comes and goes without your landing a pilot. You call your agent and say . . .

A) "Don't worry about it."
B) "Maybe I should lay off the sauce?"
C) "Okay, the tattoo on my face was a bad idea."
D) "I think it's time I made a change."

ANSWER: D—When in doubt, fire your agent.

3. You're writing a sitcom for the Fox network. You need to add a next-door neighbor. He should be . . .

A) Wacky
B) Black
C) Controversial
D) Zany

ANSWER: A—It's a sitcom law. The next-door neighbor is always wacky.

4. You're the president of a major TV network. One of your most successful and beloved talk show stars retires after thirty years on the air! You need to find a replacement pronto. You . . .

A) Replace him with the highly rated and hilarious talk show host who followed him at 12:30 for ten years.

B) Make the mildly amusing guest host the permanent host.

C) Based on a dream you had, hire the executive producer of a rundown late-night comedy show to find some nice kid to fill the largest pair of empty shoes in television.

D) Panic and call Chevy's agent.

ANSWER: D—Dana Carvey passed.

5. You've been offered a lead role in a dopey sitcom for FOX called, *One Big Happy Family*. At the same time, a brilliant new playwright asks you to take a large role in a Broadway production of his guaranteed-to-win-the-Pulitzer play. You . . .

A) Pass on the sitcom, fly to New York.

B) Thank the playwright, but accept the sitcom.

C) Ask FOX to delay the sitcom so you can do both.

D) Use the leverage of the play to get FOX to pony up another half-mil for the sitcom.

ANSWER: D—What's Broadway pay? $3.50 an hour?

6. The *National Enquirer* has printed nude photos of you romping on the beach with Daryl Hannah. You . . .

A) Ask if you can get copies of the originals to hang in your rec room.

B) Sue to keep your names in the headlines.

C) Quietly say a prayer of thanks they never found that video of you in Michael Jackson's bathtub.

D) Cancel your subscription.

ANSWER: C—No matter what they catch you at, you've done worse.

10 POINTS FOR EACH CORRECT ANSWER:

0-10 pts. . . . Actor

10-20 pts. . . . Writer

30-40 pts. . . . Producer

50 pts. . . . Barbra Streisand

60 pts. . . . President of NBC

Dear Calvert,
I'm a young, attractive, sensual woman whose sexual desires are being ignored...

...I would do anything to just experience the passion and thrill of sex again.
Signed,
Frustrated.
ADVICE IS NEVER CHEAP!
MAIL
MAIL

KNOCK KNOCK

CAL-CO
HOME

HEY! THAT'S MY WIFE!

Romance

Since I am a fabulously handsome, rich, and famous television actor, the distaff side has always found me an irresistible sexual smorgasbord. Can you blame them? However, as hard as this might be to believe, I wasn't always the buffed-out stud voted *People* magazine's Sexiest Man Alive. When I was still a puppy, I was shy and awkward around broads. It was only after years of practice—and a couple of painful experiences in the navy during the war—that I developed my patentable techniques for bedding the object of your desire.

Most of the human race has a hard time talking to the opposite sex; the hell with actually getting someone to go home with you. So, if there's any chance the species will survive, I'm going to have to give you a few pointers in the romance department.

How to Tell a Good Date...

Good Date

The Movies

Amusement Park

A Baseball Game

The Beach

A Picnic

Dancing

A Walk

Her Mom's House

An Elvis Costello Concert

Paris

Drive-In Movie

...From a Bad Date

Bad Date

- The Morgue
- Auto Salvage Yard
- A Mets Game
- The Bowery
- A Porno Show
- Dumpster Diving
- A Wake
- Your Mom's House
- An Abbott and Costello Movie
- Reykjavik
- Drive-By Shooting

Dear Cal,
My boyfriend spends an awful lot of time on overnight "business" trips. How can I tell if he's fooling around?

Diane Painter
Philadelphia, PA

From the desk of
Calvert DeForest

Dear Diane,

I believe it was Mrs. Thomas Edison who asked, "How many guys does it take to screw in a lightbulb? One; a guy will screw anything!" Of course he's fooling around! But don't get mad; get even. Sleep with his best friends.

Cheap Ways for Women to Get Lucky

The cheapest way I know to get lucky is to rent a 99-cent film, get them back to your place and go for it! Tips for guys: rent any movie that's romantic, she'll think you "sooo sensitive" and get all mushy. Try not to fall asleep, just think about what you'll get later on.

Tips for ladies, you'll have to put more thought into it. (Face it, guys have no taste when it comes to flicks.) Here's some advice to get you on the right track picking a flick to get your man. Good luck!

Videos to Get Lucky By (For Women)

Faces of Death

It will turn your stomach and you'll be humiliated at the video store if anyone you know sees it in your hand, but guys love splatter flicks, and this sucker's the granddaddy of them all. Once the intestines start flying, so will his pants.

Cartoons

Let's face it, men are basically morons. Cartoons are brightly colored, the stories are simple, and they're only about seven minutes long (the average attention span of the modern American male).

A Three Stooges Festival

It's going to get on your nerves, especially when he pokes you in the eye for the fifteenth time. Still, men like to see other men bash each other over the head with crowbars. Nobody did it better than the Stooges. If your man is a college boy, rent the one where Moe played Hitler. He'll appreciate the political satire.

Cindy Crawford's Workout Video

This isn't technically a movie. However, if you want to guarantee there's lead in his pencil, a sweaty supermodel is just the ticket.

AAU
USA

Where to Meet Men

- ♂ The men's room
- ♂ RuPaul's house
- ♂ The porno section at your local video store
- ♂ Personal ad in the back of *Guns and Ammo*
- ♂ Home Depot
- ♂ A Village People concert
- ♂ Prison
- ♂ Go-go bar (only if you're into married men)
- ♂ Star Trek convention
- ♂ Madonna's bedroom

Where to Meet Women

- The classifieds
- Plastic surgeon's waiting room
- A Susan Powter seminar
- Tattoo parlor
- Wet T-shirt contest
- Hagen Däaz
- My house
- All Men Are Rapists rally
- Madonna's bedroom

Strip Bar Etiquette

The lure of the brass rail. The erotic charms of the bump and grind. The heady aroma of overpriced watered-down draft beer served in cheap plastic mugs. Yes, the once lowly strip joint has suddenly been reborn in the nineties. Almost every major city, and plenty of crappy little ones too, now feature upscale flesh halls catering to young Turks with fat wallets and raging hormones.

Like dark airport lounges, the modern adult entertainment nightclub is a plush venue for drinking, smoking, eating, and gawking. Table dancing, lap dancing, topless shoeshines, and private shows are just a few of the many exotic and erotic services available to the customer. It's a far cry from watching your sister undress through the skylight when you were a kid.

Even though the strip joint has gone legit, there are still rules that must be followed in order to avoid embarrassing and potentially brutal consequences.

Clip and Save Dos and Don'ts of Strip Bar Etiquette

- Shy? Tongue-tied around beautiful naked women? Try this opening line: "Hey, toots! I just cashed my paycheck!" The stripper hasn't been born who can resist that one.
- It's okay to give your favorite dancer your business card. It's probably not a good idea to give her your VISA card.
- It's perfectly acceptable to tell a dancer, "I think you're very attractive," as long as you don't also say, "for an old fat whore."
- If you get hungry, order a bag of peanuts. No matter how big the waitresses' breasts are, NEVER order the clams casino.
- It's okay to stand on a chair, whistle at the dancers, and shout your love for their art. It's rarely okay to stand on the bar and shout at the bartender, "How 'bout a buyback, you inbred redneck bastard!"
- The champagne served at most strip joints is not the same as the champagne served at Spago.
- It's nice when you tell a dancer, "Your legs look like fine sculpture." They hate it when you ask, "Are those your thighs or fifty pounds of cottage cheese?"

Dear Cal,
How can I keep my grandson out of strip bars?

Margaret Rozen
Tulsa, Oklahoma

From the desk of Calvert DeForest

Dear Grandma Rozen,

Find out which strip bar he frequents and get a job there. The sight of your naked, gyrating butt will keep everyone out of strip bars!

CAL

Really Cheap Things to Do That Will End Your Marriage

- Marry someone else.
- Fill the house with Franklin Mint Kenny Rogers collector plates.
- Leave your husband and kids to travel with Snoop Doggy Dogg.
- Keep saying, "You know, Loni Anderson's single again."
- Tape a Knicks game over your wedding video.
- Keep saying, "Boy, you're fat!"
- Hit on your mother-in-law.
- At your high school reunion, go parking with an old flame.
- Become president of the United States.

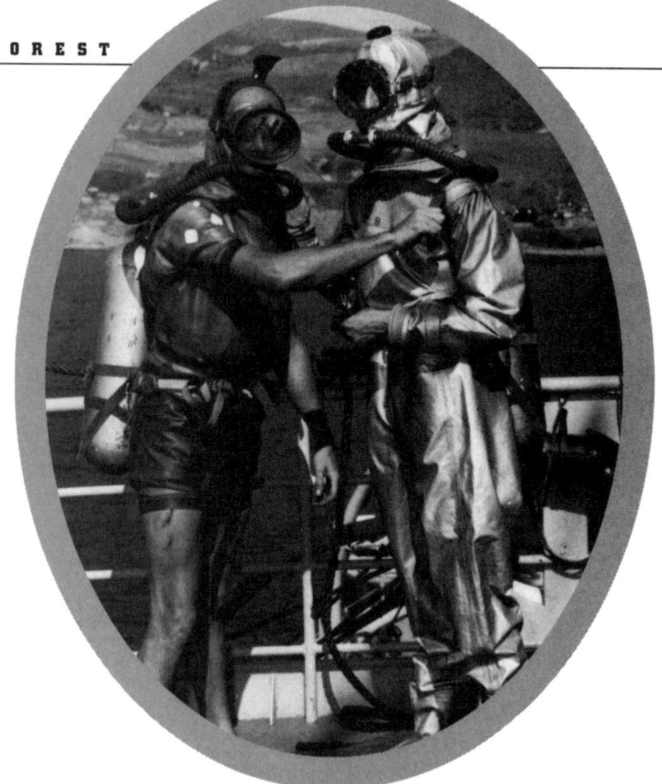

Safe Sex	Unsafe Sex
Husband and wife at home in bed	Husband and sister-in-law at home in bed
Heterosexual intercourse with a condom	Heterosexual intercourse with cactus
Teenage petting	Teenage prostitution
Hot oil massage	Boiling oil massage
Phone sex	Megaphone sex
On a waterbed	On a gas grill
In the shower	In the shower at Attica
In the kitchen	In the butt

Calvert DeForest's Advice on Choosing a Pet

It's a well-documented fact that pet owners live healthier, happier, longer lives. Those are three pretty darn good reasons to buy or trap an animal. However, don't get just any animal. Some of them make horrible pets. Some animals are wild beasts that should be left out in the woods where they can kill each other. Others are timid, nervous cowards who will sulk in their cages and provide you no companionship or entertainment value. Some animals live a very long time. (That means a lot of food.) Some animals kick the bucket before you can even think up a name for them.

A lot of people ask me, "Cal, how the heck am I going to choose the right pet?" Well, I say, of all the factors to consider when choosing a pet, there are really just two essential ones: *If this thing bites me, how much will it hurt?* and *How much does this thing crap?*

ANIMAL	BITE	CRAP
BIRDS	**3**	**2**
CATS	**5**	**2**
DOGS	**8**	**3**
ELEPHANT	**9**	**10**
GOLDFISH	**1**	**1**
GERBIL	**3**	**1**
HIPPO	**9**	**9**
JACKAL	**9**	**6**
KANGAROO	**8**	**8**
NIGHT CRAWLER	**1**	**1**
PENGUIN	**4**	**6**
SNAKE	**10**	**1**
UNICORN	**1**	**7**
WEASEL	**6**	**3**
YAK	**8**	**9**

Other factors to consider before buying a pet are:

* What are you going to do with it after it dies?
* Does it drool worse than your 86-year-old Uncle Peter?
* Lastly, in a pinch, can you sell it to Michael Jackson?

Dear Calvert,
I love my cat, Muffin, very much. However, Muffin sheds all over everything! Any suggestions?
Sincerely,
Big Mike Babette
Grand Rapids, MI

From the desk of Calvert DeForest

Dear Big Mike,
As luck would have it, Cal-Co® Industries has just introduced a brand-new pet care product—LAM-A-KAT®, the Home Cat Lamination System.

Once your kitty is encased in a thin layer of clear plastic laminate, you'll kiss that pesky shedding problem good-bye forever! And cleaning Muffin will never have been this easy. Simply spritz your cat with Windex and rub dry with a soft cloth. Ol' Muffin will be as bright and shiny as the day you brought him home.

Calvert

P.S. Lam-A-Kat® is available at pet stores everywhere, or call 1-900-SUCKERS.

Crime & Punishment

Guide to Prison Reform

American prisons have long had a reputation for being cushy country clubs where criminals go to lift weights and work on their tans. Cells with color TVs, air conditioners, wall-to-bar carpeting, free HBO, and cellular phone service . . . Hey, who do I have to kill to get a piece of this action?

If we're serious about ending our crime problems, we've got to put some teeth back into our penal system. I've got a plan: The Calvert DeForest Prison Reform Act is just what this country needs. Copy the following prison reforms and fax them to your congressman and senator:

Fence off Death Valley; let nature do its thing.
Michael Bolton CDs twenty-four hours a day.
Less appeals, more electric chairs!
Rap sessions to understand "prisioners are victims too" then fry the bastards.

Suiting the Punishment to the Crime—Cal's Way!

Column one lists selected crimes. Column two lists the current punishment for committing that crime. Column three lists what the punishment would be like if I had my way.

Crime	Current Punishment	Cal's Punishment
Auto Theft	Probation	Necklaces of Death
Burglary	Probation	Water torture
Rape	Probation	Weed Whack Their Willy
Drug Dealing	Probation	Flame Thrower
Child Pornography	Probation	Glaze Them in Honey, Tie Them to a Mound of Fire Ants
Prostitution	Probation	A Good Talking-to
Littering	Probation	Forced Sterilization
Industrial Waste	Probation	Plutonium Enema
Murder	Probation	Become a Lawyer

Art

FOR SALE

Calv-Art

What a sad and dreary place this world would be if it weren't for art! Imagine a world without paintings. A day without sunshine. A song without lyrics. An apple without razor blades!

For the first time ever, I am proud to share a few of my most personally revealing and favorite paintings with you. My art is a mirror of my soul, a complex and ever-changing reflection of my inner feelings. My paintings may have a different meaning for everyone, but one thing is certain, these powerful images will make you laugh, and they will make you cry. Feel free to look as long as you like, but please, don't touch!

60s

70s

80s
90s

ANNUAL MEETING
CAL-CO INDUSTRIES
SHARE HOLDERS

Public Speaking

How to Speak in Public

Were you the kind of kid who wet yourself every time you had to stand in front of the class to read your book report aloud? Are you the type who downs four shots of tequila every time you have to make a presentation in a sales meeting?

If you said yes to either of these questions, you should attend one of Cal-Co®'s Talk Like Cal® public speaking seminars. For only $189.99, you'll spend the afternoon in an airport hotel with me, Calvert DeForest, as I explain the secrets of my success as a public speaker.

As one of the world's most sought-after motivational speakers, I earn outrageous sums of money gabbing to Fortune 500 companies, lecturing at major universities both here and abroad, and am a regular caller to *Larry King Live*.

How many times have you heard me and said, "Why can't I talk smart like Cal?" Well, now you can. The only thing standing between you and a highly polished speaking style is a check for $189.99. Don't be a jackass, send it in today!

Spend the day with me and I'll teach you good words to use. . . . Trendy words that make you sound informed. . . . Words like "Balkanize" and "empowerment." I'll cover important topics such as "Body Language Dos and Don'ts," "How to Duck the Post-Speech Q&A Session," and, of course, hot topics like "Dick Jokes: Openers or Closers?"

Cal-Co®'s Talk Like Cal® Seminars are not available on records, tapes, or CDs. The only way to hear my pearls of wisdom is to fork over the dough and drive out to an airport Marriott. (Cheese sandwiches and Pepsi will be served at no additional cost to you.)

Consult your local paper for the Cal-Co® Talk Like Cal® Seminar nearest you, and start talking in public today!

(Offer not valid in Alaska and Hawaii. Dealer prep charges, taxes, and license not included. If I'm not there, start without me. Member FDIC.)

How to Give a Speech

Dear Calvert,

As a famous celebrity, I know you must often find yourself addressing groups of press, fans, and network executives. It looks so easy for you on television. I'm fine one-on-one, but when I have to speak to a crowd, I become paralyzed with fear. I've been asked to open my boss's anniversary dinner and I desperately need a speech! Please help!

Signed,

Guy Picca

Dumont, New Jersey

From the desk of Calvert DeForest

Dear Guy,
I've seen plenty of bright people's careers go down the crapper because of a bad performance at the lectern. I dug up a fail-safe speech. Don't bother rehearsing; you'll just get nervous trying to memorize. Actually, don't even read it now. I'd be surprised if this performance doesn't get you a corner office and a key to the executive toilet.

THE FAIL-SAFE SPEECH

It's a great honor to be here to roast (insert boss's name here).

I came here to heap words of praise upon ______ but I can't think of any, so I'll just have to tell the truth! What can be said about ______ that hasn't already been said about sexually transmitted disease? ______ really means a lot to people . . . but then again, so does Preparation H! ______ is one stupid, arrogant, bottom feeder . . . and those are ______'s good qualities! Instead of being in Who's Who, ______ is in What the Hell Is That?! Popular? As a kid ______ had plenty of friends. Then ______'s father stopped paying them! Talk about stupid . . . the reason ______ doesn't watch championship wrestling is 'cause ______ can't follow the plot! Stupid? When I asked, "Have you ever used a Dictaphone?" ______ said, "No, I use my finger like everyone else." I want ______ to know: If I have said anything here that might have offended you, I sure tried hard enough!

Screw you, and good luck, sucker! HA! HA! HA!

PHYSICS

School

CALCULUS

How to Pick the Right College

- Find a college that is academically demanding and intellectually stimulating. Find out what school they make fun of. Go there.
- Don't go to a school that always produces Rhodes Scholars, but never produces "Babes of the Big East."
- Don't believe anything a college admissions director tells you if the school's administration building is a Winnebago.
- Go to any school that offers a massage major.
- Be wary of any college recruiter who says, "Let's talk about your future over drinks at my place."
- University of Maui. Yeah, right!
- You might want to rethink your choice if the dean of students says, "Hot damn! We never had us a colored boy before!"
- Don't trust a scholarship that requires you to use a baseball bat to pick up money from local merchants.

Really Bad Majors

- ✘ Pancake House management
- ✘ Mob informing
- ✘ High school custodianship
- ✘ Creative capital punishment
- ✘ Customer service representation
- ✘ Embezzlement
- ✘ Tobacco Marketing
- ✘ Squeegee Guy
- ✘ Sleeping and drinking (some schools offer as double major)
- ✘ Cult leadership

Choosing the Right Major

College is that golden four-year adventure of learning, maturation, sexual awakening, and recreational drug use. It's that time of life when you spend great sums of your parent's money to attend classes on important subjects like:

- "Living Off Dad"
- "Creative Writing . . . Home for Money"
- "Converting Text Books to Cash"
- "Golf"

Calvert,
I'm a student here at George Washington U, and I'm a huge-HUGE fan, dude. My problem is I can't decide between spending a hundred and fifty dollars on textbooks or the new Pearl Jam live box set. What do you suggest?

Steven Puglisi
Hewlitt Hall

From the desk of
Calvert DeForest

Dear Steven,
Boy, you really are hopeless! How the hell do you expect to lure babes back to your boudoir with books on ethics? Stay in college; a knucklehead like you shouldn't be operating heavy equipment.

How to Get a 4.0

- Study.
- Get a brain transplant.
- Sleep with the professor.
- Pay me to sleep with the professor's wife.
- Plant incriminating evidence on the professor.
- Seduce the computer operator in the dean's office.
- Learn how to throw a football seventy-five yards on the money.
- Remind the dean that the library was a gift from your dad.
- Go to a crappy college where grade inflation is out of control.
- Cheat.

Cheating

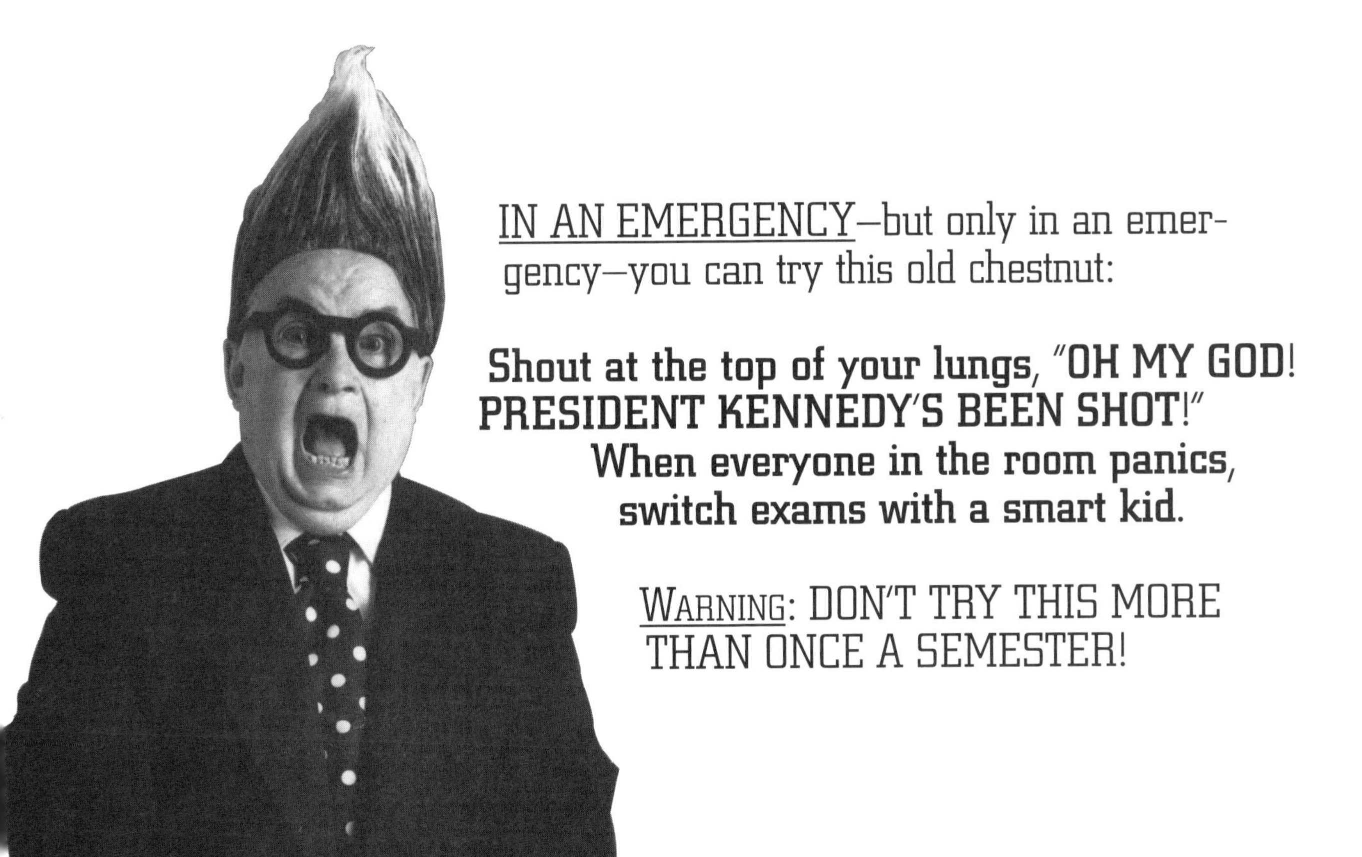

IN AN EMERGENCY—but only in an emergency—you can try this old chestnut:

Shout at the top of your lungs, "OH MY GOD! PRESIDENT KENNEDY'S BEEN SHOT!" When everyone in the room panics, switch exams with a smart kid.

WARNING: DON'T TRY THIS MORE THAN ONCE A SEMESTER!

Great Places to Spend Spring Break

- Amsterdam.
- All expense paid vacation with "Miss Hawaiian Tropic."
- Mel Gibson's hot-tub.
- Taunting last year's graduates working the drive-through window at McDonald's.
- At the nightclub with an entire roll of drink tickets you found.
- Ted Kennedy's wine cellar.
- In a brand-new Viper with your roommate's life insurance money.
- Puking your lungs out from the hotel balcony.
- Directing the *Sports Illustrated* swimsuit issue.
- Throwing the switch on Florida's death row.

Bad Places to Spend Spring Break

- Pauley Shore's *Spring Break Pow-Wow '95!*
- In a casket
- The library
- The Department of Motor Vehicles
- At home with Dad watching C-Span
- Prison
- In traffic
- The Betty Ford Clinic
- Chained to a radiator
- Cher's bedroom

DEAR CAL,
I'M COMPLETELY BROKE! I DESPERATELY NEED THE MONEY I GAVE YOU! PLEASE HELP ME OR I'LL END IT ALL!!!
SLEEP PILLS

THE ADVICE GOD IS IN

SUCKER.

Advice

Cal's Cheap Advice on Advice

I believe it was my attorney who said, "Advice is cheap, but it ain't free." The problem with you people is you don't understand the difference between advice and an opinion. I can't tell you the number of times I've had some poor slob come up to me and say, "Cal, what do you think of this suit?" I always say the same thing—"Is the circus in town?" HA! HA! HA! Sure, men cry and women slap my face, but screw 'em; they asked for an opinion. You see, an opinion can't be wrong, but advice can.

So, when it comes to giving advice, my advice is: *Don't*. It's not as easy as it looks. You people should just go about your drab little lives and leave the advice game to someone like me, a professional! If my advice helps you just once in your life, then I've done my job.

Final Words of Wisdom

Thank you, and remember these final words of wisdom:

- ✔ Don't take wooden nickels.
- ✔ Don't run with scissors.
- ✔ Wait an hour after eating before entering the pool.
- ✔ Get the hell off the golf course in a thunderstorm!
- ✔ Wear sensible shoes.
- ✔ Look both ways before crossing the street.
- ✔ Avoid snacks between meals.
- ✔ Don't buy the cow when the milk is so cheap.
- ✔ Send Calvert DeForest all your money.

LIVE IT UP; IT'S LATER THAN YOU THINK!

Other Books by the Author

If you enjoyed this Calvert DeForest book, you're sure to enjoy these:

Calvert DeForest's Civil War Diaries

Cal's Really Private Parts

The Escape from the Return to Planet of the Apes III

The DeForest Way to a Total Body Perfection in 90 Days!

The Holy Bible